Greater Than a T
Reviews fr

I think the series is wonderful and beneficial for tourists to get information before visiting the city.

-Seckin Zumbul, Izmir Turkey

I am a world traveler who has read many trip guides but this one really made a difference for me. I would call it a heartfelt creation of a local guide expert instead of just a guide.

-Susy, Isla Holbox, Mexico

New to the area like me, this is a must have!

-Joe, Bloomington, USA

This is a good series that gets down to it when looking for things to do at your destination without having to read a novel for just a few ideas.

-Rachel, Monterey, USA

Good information to have to plan my trip to this destination.

-Pennie Farrell, Mexico

Great ideas for a port day.
-Mary Martin USA

Stephen Philips

Aptly titled, you won't just be a tourist after reading this book. You'll be greater than a tourist!

-Alan Warner, Grand Rapids, USA

Thank you for a fantastic book.

-Don, Philadelphia, USA

Even though I only have three days to spend in San Miguel in an upcoming visit, I will use the author's suggestions to guide some of my time there. An easy read - with chapters named to guide me in directions I want to go.

-Robert Catapano, USA

Great insights from a local perspective! Useful information and a very good value!

-Sarah, USA

This series provides an in-depth experience through the eyes of a local. Reading these series will help you to travel the city in with confidence and it'll make your journey a unique one.

-Andrew Teoh, Ipoh, Malaysia

>TOURIST

GREATER THAN A TOURIST – GIBRALTAR

50 Travel Tips from a Local

Stephen Philips

Stephen Philips

Greater Than a Tourist- Gibraltar Copyright © 2018 by CZYK Publishing LLC.
All Rights Reserved.

All rights reserved. No part of this book may be reproduced in any form or by any electronic or mechanical means including information storage and retrieval systems, without permission in writing from the author. The only exception is by a reviewer, who may quote short excerpts in a review.

Cover designed by: Ivana Stamenković
Cover Image: https://pixabay.com/en/gibraltar-rock-aerial-view-panorama-2079953/

Edited by:

Greater Than a Tourist
Visit our website at www.GreaterThanaTourist.com

Lock Haven, PA
All rights reserved.

ISBN: 9781980771401

>TOURIST

>TOURIST
50 TRAVEL TIPS FROM A LOCAL

Stephen Philips

>TOURIST
BOOK DESCRIPTION

Are you excited about planning your next trip?

Do you want to try something new?

Would you like some guidance from a local?

If you answered yes to any of these questions, then this Greater Than a Tourist book is for you.

Greater Than a Tourist- Gibraltar by Stephen Philips offers the inside scoop on Gibraltar. Most travel books tell you how to travel like a tourist. Although there is nothing wrong with that, as part of the Greater Than a Tourist series, this book will give you travel tips from someone who has lived at your next travel destination.

In these pages, you will discover advice that will help you throughout your stay. This book will not tell you exact addresses or store hours but instead will give you excitement and knowledge from a local that you may not find in other smaller print travel books.

Travel like a local. Slow down, stay in one place, and get to know the people and the culture. By the time you finish this book, you will be eager and prepared to travel to your next destination.

Stephen Philips

>TOURIST

TABLE OF CONTENTS

BOOK DESCRIPTION
TABLE OF CONTENTS
DEDICATION
ABOUT THE AUTHOR
HOW TO USE THIS BOOK
FROM THE PUBLISHER
OUR STORY
WELCOME TO
> TOURIST
INTRODUCTION
1. Arrive By Air
2. Stop At The Runway To Watch An Aeroplane Take-off And/Or Land
3. Stop At The Cradle Of History Monument On Your Way Into Town
4. Ocean Village & Marina
5. Dolphin Safari
6. Grand Casemates Square
7. Gibraltar Crystal - Glass Blowing Exhibition
8. Moorish Castle
9. Main Street

Stephen Philips

10. Piazza
(John MacIntosh Square)
11. Commonwealth Park
12. Lovers' Lane
13. Walk Through Square from Lovers' Lane to Queensway Quay
14. Queensway Quay
15. Cable Car
16. Barbary Apes
17. Med Steps
18. St. Michael's Cave
19. Lower St. Michael's Cave
20. Go For A Spin
21. Speak Llanito
22. Europa Point
23. Gibraltar Museum
24. 100 Tonne Gun
25. Sandy Beach
26. Polar Bear Swim
27. Alameda Gardens
28. King's Bastion
29. The Convent
30. Feria
31. Great Siege Tunnels
32. Evacuation Monument

33. Nelson's Anchorage
34. Gorham's Cave Complex
35. O'Hara's Battery
36. Chatham Counterguard
37. Gibraltar Public Market
38. Skywalk
39. Star Bar
40. Bobby on the Beat
41. Red Telephone Boxes
42. Europort
43. American Steps
44. Windsor Suspension Bridge
45. Pillars Of Hercules Monument
46. Tax Free Goods
47. Local Dish
48. Casinos
49. Live Music & Music Festival
50. Three Kings' Cavalcade

TOP REASONS TO BOOK THIS TRIP

50 THINGS TO KNOW ABOUT PACKING LIGHT FOR TRAVEL

> TOURIST

GREATER THAN A TOURIST

> TOURIST

GREATER THAN A TOURIST

Stephen Philips

NOTES

>TOURIST

DEDICATION

This book is dedicated to Alex & Eric with the hope that it ignites in them a passion for travel and discovery.

Stephen Philips

ABOUT THE AUTHOR

Stephen Philips lives in Gibraltar. Stephen loves to travel, pass on tips that he has learned throughout his own journeys moving around Europe; living in several different countries. Passionate about Gibraltar and its people, this book is written in the hope that it encourages you to visit The Rock, which is truly a one of a kind location; routinely stereotyped and overlooked and well worth the visit.

Stephen Philips

>TOURIST

HOW TO USE THIS BOOK

The Greater Than a Tourist book series was written by someone who has lived in an area for over three months. The goal of this book is to help travelers either dream or experience different locations by providing opinions from a local. The author has made suggestions based on their own experiences. Please do your own research before traveling to the area in case the suggested places are unavailable.

Stephen Philips

FROM THE PUBLISHER

Traveling can be one of the most important parts of a person's life. The anticipation and memories that you have are some of the best. As a publisher of the Greater Than a Tourist book series, as well as the popular 50 Things to Know book series, we strive to help you learn about new places, spark your imagination, and inspire you. Wherever you are and whatever you do I wish you safe, fun, and inspiring travel.

Lisa Rusczyk Ed. D.
CZYK Publishing

Stephen Philips

OUR STORY

Traveling is a passion of the "Greater than a Tourist" series creator. Lisa studied abroad in college, and for their honeymoon Lisa and her husband toured Europe. During her travels to Malta, an older man tried to give her some advice based on his own experience living on the island since he was a young boy. She was not sure if she should talk to the stranger but was interested in his advice. When traveling to some places she was wary to talk to locals because she was afraid that they weren't being genuine. Through her travels, Lisa learned how much locals had to share with tourists. Lisa created the "Greater Than a Tourist" book series to help connect people with locals. A topic that locals are very passionate about sharing.

Stephen Philips

WELCOME TO
> TOURIST

Stephen Philips

>TOURIST

INTRODUCTION

*"Travel is fatal to prejudice,
bigotry and narrowmindedness"*

-Mark Twain

When I first laid eyes on Gibraltar, I knew I had stumbled upon a place like no other. Located at the crossroads where Europe meets Africa and the Atlantic meets the Mediterranean, Gibraltar is a limestone rocky outcrop at the southern tip of the Iberian Peninsula. Jutting out of the sea, the Rock forms an imposing landscape that looks to be a little out of place; appearing to have been picked up and dropped where Iberia slips away into the sea. This contradiction of topography is echoed throughout every aspect of Gibraltar, which I hope that this guide will go some way to celebrate. Though an overseas territory of the United Kingdom with a distinctly British feel; the stamp of its Spanish and Arabic history is evident in its architecture and people. Whilst the Rock may be viewed as old fashioned or out of touch, it is home to

Stephen Philips

some of the most modern and innovative industries and, whilst it is no secret that the native Gibraltarian population is immensely proud of their British status, rather than be insular and in spite of ongoing political debate as to the future sovereignty of the Rock, it is explicit in its pride to be European and embraces its Spanish heritage rather than attempting to surpress its influence. A nation of historical and geographical importance and a modern melting pot that remains both charming and cosmopolitan; Gibraltar is a unique place to visit and, although only 6.7 km2 or 2.6 square miles in size, is full of experiences to be had or sights to be seen.   Here are fifty things to do when you arrive:

>TOURIST

Stephen Philips

>TOURIST

1. Arrive By Air

Touted as the most dangerous airport in Europe, arriving in Gibraltar by air can be an experience (especially in winter when cross winds around the Rock can be particularly blustery). If the approach is too dangerous, you'll find yourself diverted to Malaga airport; a two hour drive away along the Costa del Sol in Spain but, if conditions are favourable and, more often than not they are, the first thing that you'll notice is that, at either end of the runway, is the Mediterranean Sea. The second thing that will grab your attention is that, running straight through the middle of the runway is Winston Churchill Avenue: The only road in and out of Gibraltar, which happens to be a four-lane highway. Note you will typically require a UK connection to fly to Gibraltar.

I have been on board inbound flights in winter on more than one occasion which have struggled to land and often the pilot will attempt more than one landing in order to avoid the diversion to Malaga. Three times is my personal record at attempting to land before aborting and heading down the coast and, as the plane accelerated and began to climb once more I found myself torn between preferring to endure the time that landing in Malaga and being ferried down the coast in coaches takes and wanting to make one last try to touchdown on the Rock.

That said, the vast majority of landings happen on the first try and arrivals and departures are somewhat uneventful. The convenience of walking into the airport within ten minutes of leaving the city is not to be sniffed at and makes it worth risking the diversion in the windier of the winter months.

2. Stop At The Runway To Watch An Aeroplane Take-off And/Or Land

Whether you have arrived by air, land or sea, the fact that the road in and out of the Rock is closed so that aeroplanes are able to land and leave is a must see. The Gibraltar Police coordinate the road closure; first for pedestrians and subsequently for cyclists, motorists as well as the border workers that cross from Spain on

>TOURIST

skateboards, skates, scooters; all manner of things to make their journey more expedient, since border queues, particularly to exit the Rock, can be unpredictable. Within ten minutes, a passenger jet will pass before your very eyes completing or beginning its journey to or from Gibraltar.

The airport has a viewing deck, which you're able to enter without the need for a plane ticket by entering the terminal and turning right. The gallery spans the length of the airport, however, meaning those who are departing on flights are also able to take advantage of the views, once they are checked in and through security. From here you can take a stunning picture of a passenger jet taking off with the Rock itself serving as a dramatic back drop.

Stephen Philips

3. Stop At The Cradle Of History Monument On Your Way Into Town

Walking across the runway, when there are no jets in sight, from the direction of Spain to Gibraltar; you'll want to be on the right-hand side and, on your right, just before you cross the runway completely, you'll see a monument welcoming you to Gibraltar; the Cradle of History. The monument is in the form of the Rock, details the historical importance of Gibraltar and makes a great backdrop for a photograph. As you're walking across the runway, you also have the perfect, uninterrupted view of the Rock that you will see in John Lennon & Yoko Ono's wedding pictures, although you will want to be on the left-hand side of the runway in order to avoid traffic spoiling your photo. Please bear in mind when crossing roads that, although distinctly British, Gibraltarians drive on the right-hand side of the road and be quick whilst taking your photographs! Any pedestrians caught straggling whilst they cross the live runway will be told unceremoniously over a tannoy system to keep on moving.

4. Ocean Village & Marina

Ocean Village is a residential, office, and primarily leisure area of Gibraltar; filled with shops, bars and restaurants. Friday nights can get particularly lively (with Saturdays usually being decidedly quiet, since the tradition is to cross the border and go out in Spain on Saturdays). Bars are open throughout the day, right from breakfast time and there are nightclubs that will take you through to breakfast the following day. The annual Cardboard Boat Race in August takes place in the waters here and calendar events such as St. Patrick's Day in March are celebrated with great gusto here. Many of the bars have happy hours that coincide with the end of the business day, where you will find cross border workers from all over Europe unwinding after a hard day in the office; speaking a multitude of languages and switching from one to another. Be aware that in several of the bars, late into the evening, resident photographers will be working the room, taking snaps of their patrons, which will be uploaded to their social media pages.

5. Dolphin Safari

There are several companies offering trips out into the Strait of Gibraltar, towards the Moroccan coastline, where there's as close to a guarantee as possible that you are going to see pods of wild dolphins. If you don't get to see any of these wild mammals, a free return trip is usually offered and there is also the possibility of seeing whales (although no guarantee is offered of this). The distance between Gibraltar and Morocco is only approximately fourteen kilometres or nine miles so the trip alone is worth it to see the Rif mountains of the North African coast rising high above you. When I took this trip, the launch coincided with the taking off of a plane so we waited at the end of the runway whilst the aeroplane took off directly over our heads. As soon as we moved out into the Strait, we were accompanied by dolphins, which didn't leave our side until we returned back to the marina.

>TOURIST

6. Grand Casemates Square

One of the principal sights of Gibraltar and the setting for Gibraltar's New Year festivities, Casemates has to be on your checklist. As well as the new police station, you'll find shops, cafes, bars and restaurants galore; all with terraces that are perfect for people watching. A Christmas Tree dominates the square during the festive season and open-air concerts take place here throughout the year. Historically, the square has been a beach as well as the site of public executions but nowadays, the atmosphere is decidedly more jovial. On Gibraltar's National Day, 10th September, you could be forgiven for thinking that the entire population of the Rock descends upon the Square for what is always the focus of celebrations.

7. Gibraltar Crystal - Glass Blowing Exhibition

Situated in Casemates, next to the arches that lead you to the bus station and market, you'll find Gibraltar Crystal. You'll recognise it as there's an ideal photo opportunity with a life-size model of a glass blower outside the front door. With a free exhibition on glass blowing and the chance to see pieces being made on-site, it's a great place to pick up locally made souvenirs.

8. Moorish Castle

Halfway up the Rock, its Tower of Homage clearly visible across the border in Spain, you'll see Gibraltar's Moorish Castle. Constructed in the 8th Century, the walk up to the castle from Casemates can be murder on your legs but the views of the city are your reward for making the vertical journey. Parts of the castle used to the house prisoners, up until 2010 but the only other people you will see is the handful of tourists that have braved the climb up to this vantage point, the construction of which began in the 8th Century. At

>TOURIST

night, the castle is lit up in numerous colours to reflect various events: red and white on National Day for example: the colours of the flag of Gibraltar and the uniform for anyone celebrating National Day on 10th September.

9. Main Street

Running from Grand Casemate's Square and leading you up towards the Cable Car Station, Main Street is the principal shopping street of Gibraltar. A pedestrianised zone, lined with all kinds of shops, pubs and, as you get further away from Casemates, bistros. You'll also find one of Gibraltar's cathedrals here; the Roman Catholic Cathedral of St. Mary the Crowned. Located on the left-hand side of the street, as you walk with Casemates behind you, you cannot miss this huge 15th Century construction. When cruise ships are in town, and often more than one can be docked at the same time, Main Street can become pretty crowded. If you're in a hurry to get from one end of the centre to the other, make like a local and take the parallel-running street Irish Town which, although decidedly lacking in anything Irish, is a much quieter thoroughfare and will get you from Point A to Point B much more quickly. Taxi ranks are able to be found at the northern end of the street, where it joins Grand Casemates Square and also towards the southern end of the Street, just behind the Cathedral of the Holy Trinity.

The Cathedral of the Holy Trinity is the Church of England cathedral of Gibraltar, located in Cathedral Square and built in a Moorish style. Built between 1825 and 1832, it is yellow and white and has the typical Moorish horseshoe arches at its main entrance.

10. Piazza (John MacIntosh Square)

On your way to the Cathedral of St. Mary the Crowned, you will have seen Gibraltar's white Parliament building, with restaurants either side of it on your right. On the other side of this building, you will find Gibraltar's 14th Century Piazza or John Mackintosh Square. At the other end of the square, you'll find City Hall; the office of the Mayor of Gibraltar. Littered with benches that are perfect for lounging around in the sun and people watching, the

>TOURIST

square can provide welcome relief from the crowds of people that will be in Main Street. Free public conveniences are able to be found here and bars and food stalls are starting to find their way into the Square, which also hosts attractions for children from time to time.

11. Commonwealth Park

Opened in 2014, Commonwealth Park is the first public park built in Gibraltar in almost two hundred years. Surrounded by city walls and with a calming water features and fish ponds, which are also home to a number of turtles, the park is an oasis right in the heart of busy Gibraltar. The perfect place to picnic and a favourite with local families, a world music festival also takes place here once a year.

I will often come here at lunchtime and take the time to relax and refocus in order to head back to work reenergised. There is plenty of seating in the sunshine during the cooler months and also ample shade for during summer. Commonwealth Park is a great outdoors space in a place where this is of a premium and it never gets too crowded that you are unable to unwind.

12. Lovers' Lane

If you head up the stairs or lift in the centre of the back wall of the park and walk south, you will find yourself in a winding street, with a plaque detailing its past as the haunting for amorous couples. If you're travelling with your significant other, why not follow the lead of those that went before you and steal a kiss here? A word of warning, the road that now runs through here gets quite busy!

13. Walk Through Square from Lovers' Lane to Queensway Quay

As you continue south, you will note on your right-hand side a ramp leading down, that will lead you to a modern square within the old city walls, which you're then able to climb and meander. This area is not well known so it will not be unusual to find that you have it all to yourself. It's a part of Gibraltar that I really

>TOURIST

enjoy. Whilst evidently old, the area is so clean and so well maintained that it could easily be a new installation. You have the freedom to walk all over the structure, usually with nobody else around and there's something that I can't quite put my finger on which keeps me coming back to this place.

In the courtyard, you will note several inconspicuous doors. As you round the corner to your right, you need to be headed towards the one on the left, which opens up into a high vaulted square ceiling, which takes you to Queensway and a crossing into its Quay.

14. Queensway Quay

Restaurants, Bars and a slower pace to that of Ocean Village will await you at Queensway Quay. This is the perfect place to relax and unwind, take in the views of the marina and have a photograph taken on the steps at which Royal visitors have disembarked upon arrival into Gibraltar. Less common with tourists, here you'll be eating with the locals. This is another of my favourite areas in Gibraltar. It feels more exclusive than Ocean Village, mostly due to the fact that there are less people around, although the shorter height of the buildings here mean that the sun does shine that little bit longer and the standard of restaurant and service seems to be that little bit better than in other areas of Gibraltar.

15. Cable Car

The Cable Car to the Apes' Den halfway up the Rock, which then continues all the way to the top, can be found a little further on from the southern end of Main Street, next to the Alameda Botanical Gardens. Built in 1966, the cable car is probably the quickest way to get to the top of the Rock and see the famous Barbary Apes. You're able to book single or return tickets but there can sometimes be queues so it's worth getting there early.

I always prefer to be at the back of the gondola as you are climbing the Rock (or front as you are descending). Here you are best placed to enjoy the views of the Bay of Gibraltar or the Bay of Algeciras as it is also known.

At the top station, you'll find the macaques, a souvenir shop and a café as well as spectacular, uninterrupted panoramic views.

16. Barbary Apes

Visiting Gibraltar and not visiting the only wild colony of Macaques in Europe is not an option. An emblem of the Rock and a feature on the local coins, legend has it that when the barbary macaques leave Gibraltar, so too will British control end. That said, their presence in the Rock is documented long before the arrival of the British.

Remember that these are wild animals and, whilst not aggressive, they are drawn to shiny items and will assume that any plastic bag contains food and will make an attempt to secure the contents for themselves.

If you're an a Rock Tour and decide to stay in your taxi or coach in order to avoid an encounter with the Apes, I have seen one jump from the trees to the roof of the car and enter the minibus much to the horror of the occupant with a phobia of the monkeys, who pressed herself against the rear window of the vehicle; screaming as though it was something much more frightening than a macaque coming towards her. The uninvited guest did vacate the vehicle without getting any closer to the lady in question.

I myself have fallen victim to the apes on one occasion. After having been caving in Lower St. Michael's Cave, I was changing out of my wet clothes in the small car park that is outside of the cave's entrance; my dry clothes in a plastic bag in the boot of my car. As indicated above, for the apes, plastic bags equal food and I found myself chasing after the monkey who stole my change of clothes out of my car, whilst wearing only my underpants. Unlike myself (prior to my impromptu exhibitionism), the barbary macaques are not shy.

17. Med Steps

Another way to get to the summit of the Rock is on foot. The Med Steps run from Martin's Path to Lord Airey's Battery and are located squarely in the Upper Rock Nature Reserve. Recently renovated, the route is

>TOURIST

fairly safe, though some of the steps are fairly steep and the climb is not for the faint-hearted. The panoramic views from the top of the Rock make the effort worthwhile, however. Should your visit coincide with the annual Med Steps Challenge, why not join in and complete the climb five times in one day in order to raise money for charity?

The route is a favourite amongst locals and I understand that the record for scaling the Steps stands around the fifteen minute mark. I myself have come nowhere near this time since, each time that I have 'done' the Mediterranean Steps, I've been with friends who have been doing it for the first time, who stop several times along the way to take selfies with the Bay behind them.

18. St. Michael's Cave

The Rock of Gibraltar is riddled with caves, so much so that I have heard it likened to a lump of Swiss cheese. St. Michael's Cave is arguably the most famous and certainly the most visited of these caves. As well as all of the stalactites and stalagmites and other cave formations that you would expect to see, you will find an auditorium, stage included, which regularly hosts shows and concerts. The lighting and acoustics in the Cathedral Cave chamber make for an unforgettable evening's entertainment should your stay coincide with an event.

19. Lower St. Michael's Cave

Whilst it's possible to turn up to St. Michael's Cave unannounced and gain entry, entrance to the Lower St. Michael's Cave must be arranged in advance with specialist guides. There's some climbing and squeezing in small spaces involved but, should you be fine to negotiate the more natural state of this cave, you'll be rewarded with the sight of a clear, underground lake; long believed to be bottomless, the opening of a passageway under the Strait into Africa and even an entrance to the Underworld.

If you arrange the visit, you will not be disappointed and all safety gear will be provided to you. When I have visited the caves, I have been with people with zero experience in caving or rock climbing and who are

>TOURIST

not sporty at all and all have managed to complete the tour without too much difficulty. You will have the cave all to yourselves so I would encourage anybody thinking about organizing a visit to do so.

20. Go For A Spin

A truly Gibraltarian pastime, going for a spin is driving all the way around the Rock. Reserved for outside of rush hour, when traffic can be particularly bad, the route will take you on a circuit of Gibraltar and inside the Rock itself where you'll see some fantastic views of the Strait, of the east side of the rock when you emerge from the Dudley Ward road tunnel that you entered just after Europa Point.

A tip for you, should you have driven into Gibraltar and find yourself in a particularly lengthy border queue, it's possible to bypass much of the traffic by driving around the Rock and joining the queue in Devil's Tower Road, into which heavy traffic is diverted when the wait to leave Gibraltar is long.

21. Speak Llanito

Llanito is the local name for Gibraltarian and refers to the language as well as the people. Having just been for a spin around the Rock, it's only right that you start communicating like a local, using a mixture of English and Spanish. You'll hear sentences that start in one language and finish in the other, whole conversations punctuated with 'pleases' and 'thank yous'. It's a great environment for practicing any school day Spanish that you can remember.

22. Europa Point

At the southern tip of Gibraltar, you'll find Europa Point. You'll need to take a bus or taxi to get here should you not be driving, where you will find ample parking should you have your own vehicle. There are a few things to see at Europa Point: The Ibrahim-al-Ibrahim Mosque, for example. The mosque is also known as the Mosque of the Custodian of the Two Holy Mosques or the King Fahd bin Abdulaziz al-Saud Mosque. The King Fahd bin Abdulaziz al-Saud name stems from the fact that the building is a gift from King

>TOURIST

Fahd of Saudi Arabia. Inaugerated in 1997, the building is the southern-most mosque in continental Europe, took two years to build and came in at a cost of circa five million pounds.

In addition to the mosque, there is a university campus of the University of Gibraltar, which was founded in 2015. The university caters to local industries and offers courses in Finance, Law and Business Administration but, for the vast majority of Gibraltarian undergraduates looking to go on to Higher Education, the United Kingdom is their destination.

Possibly the most famous landmark at Europa Point is the iconic red and white Europa Point Trinity House Lighthouse. A feature on the local two pence coin, the lighthouse stands twenty metres tall and has been in service since 1841.

At Europa Point, you will be standing literally at the edge of the Rock and the sea views across the Strait are fantastic. That said, turn your back on the Mediterranean for a moment and you also have dramatic views of the south west of the Rock.

23. Gibraltar Museum

Tucked away in a back street which runs off Main Street, you will find the Gibraltar Museum in Bomb House Lane. Here you will learn all about the history of Gibraltar and the museum incorporates the remains of a 14th Century Moorish bath house. This is a good option for a rainy day and it is amazing to learn how a place so small can have such a diverse history and have been fought over so many times, arguably until this day.

24. 100 Tonne Gun

Built in Britain in 1870 as one of four guns designed to fend off enemy designs on both Gibraltar and Malta, the 100 Tonne Gun, located at the Napier of Magdala Battery is one of a pair of surviving cannons (the other remaining on the island of Malta). With a barrel measuring almost ten metres and a range of almost thirteen kilometres, in its day, the 100 Tonne Gun (which actually weighs a little more than 100 tonnes) was the pinnacle of weaponary.

>TOURIST

25. Sandy Beach

Whilst the beaches of Gibraltar and the Costa del Sol have relatively dark sands, which can get rather hot under foot during summer, the sands of Sandy Beach are golden sands, imported from Loyounne in the Western Sahara. Billed as one of the best beaches in Gibraltar, if you're able to find a spot, it's well worth the trip around to the eastern side of the Rock to catch some sun. Unlike the western side of the Rock, which is in shadow for the early part of the day, Sandy Beach has sun from the moment it rises.

26. Polar Bear Swim

Every year on Boxing Day (26th December), Catalan Bay on the east coast of Gibraltar is the venue for the Polar Bear Swim. The waters around Gibraltar are cool all year round, with the Atlantic feeding into the Mediterranean, so hats off to those of you who are open to going for a lunch time dip into the sea during winter. Surprisingly, this event draws quite the crowd and, once you've had enough of the cold waves, there are usually warm refreshments on hand in the form of mulled wine and mince pies to help recover.

27. Alameda Gardens

Established in 1816, the Alameda Gardens have been providing locals with a sanctuary from the heat of summer for two hundred years. Located next to the Cable Car ground station, here you'll enjoy a variety of flora, a myriad of wildlife, sculpture and even an open-air theatre. Located within the gardens, the Alameda Wildlife Conservation Park is a small zoo, which children will especially find appealing.

28. King's Bastion

King's Bastion is an 18th Century military fortress that now houses a cinema, bowling alley, amusement arcade, gym, restaurants, bars and an ice rink. Located next to Midtown and Commonwealth Park, it's a great place to spend an evening or an afternoon out of the heat of the summer sun (especially the ice rink). As the only cinema in town, new films can easily sell out, so it is worth considering buying your tickets in advance.

>TOURIST

29. The Convent

Towards the southernly end of Main Street (the opposite end to Casemates), you will find the official residence of the Governor of Gibraltar. Built in the 16th Century, the building takes its name from its former incarnation as a convent. Guarded by the Royal Gibraltar Regiment, the building has two cannons facing it on the opposite side of the road, which make for a good souvenir photograph.

30. Feria

The position and history of Gibraltar sees many Spanish traditions cross over the frontier, including the passion for the feria. The feris or fair is something that is taken very seriously in Iberia and for one week in August, the fair comes to town in Gibraltar. As well as the traditional fairground rides, entertainment is scheduled throughout the week.

41

31. Great Siege Tunnels

The Great Siege Tunnels or Upper Galleries were mostly carved out of the Rock by hand (aided by the occasional gun powder blast) by the British when French and Spanish forces laid siege to Gibraltar from 1779 to 1783; the longest siege ever endured by the British army. The Great Siege was the fourteenth and final in Gibraltar's history. You'll see the tunnel openings as you approach Gibraltar from Spain. Guns were placed at the end of each opening, targeting advancing enemy troops.

32. Evacuation Monument

During World War II, much of the Gibraltarian civilian population was evacuated from the Rock, which was instead populated by British Armed Forces. A monument to the evacuation stands on a roundabout on North Mole Road at Waterport, which you will pass if you are arriving by cruise ship on your way into town. The monument details how locals were shipped off to Morocco, the UK, Madeira and Jamaica during the war.

>TOURIST

33. Nelson's Anchorage

Nelson's Anchorage in Rosia Bay is in the same area as the 100 Tonne Gun. It is said to be, in spite of official denials, the spot where Vice-Admiral Horatio Nelson's body was brought ashore after his death at Cape Trafalgar, where he was shot and killed in his final victory in 1805 (after having lost the sight in one eye in Corsica and much of his right arm in Santa Cruz de Tenerife during a failed attempt to capture the city. Nelson (who ironically suffered with sea sickness) was allegedly brought ashore onto Gibraltar in a barrel of brandy and subsequently despatched back to England in a lead-lined coffin filled with spirits of wine.

34. Gorham's Cave Complex

A Unesco World Heritage Site since 2016, Gorham's Cave Complex is made up of four individual natural sea caves, located on the south east coast of the Rock and able to be viewed only from the sea. They are famed for their Neanderthal inhabitants and said to be the last bolt hole of our ancestors. It is possible in advance to arrange a tour by boat with one of the operators in Ocean Village, though there are no regular scheduled visits.

35. O'Hara's Battery

Located at the highest point of the Rock, at the top of the Mediterranean Steps, towards the southern end of the Upper Rock Nature Reserve, O'Hara's Battery was constructed in the late 19th Century and fitted with its first huge military guns with a twenty-five kilometre (16 miles) range after the turn of the 20th Century in 1901. The gun was last fired during a training exercise in 1976.

36. Chatham Counterguard

At the bottom of the American Steps you'll find, on turning right, a strip of bars, tapas bars and restaurants which locals like to keep for themselves. Becoming increasingly popular at both lunch and dinner times, it's worth making a reservation should you be looking for a table in any of the places on offer. The most popular offerings are to be found closer to the Steps. An annual

>TOURIST

wine festival has also recently begun to be held in this part of town.

37. Gibraltar Public Market

Next to the bus station by Casemates, you'll find the 1920s indoor covered market on your right as your about to walk through the archways into the Square. The market is well worth meandering around, whether you're looking to purchase or not. Selling fruit, fish and other foods, you'll be able to pick up a slice of locally produced fresh goods here. It's from where I buy my smoothie ingredients.

38. Skywalk

A new tourist attraction in the Upper Rock Nature Reserve, opened by the actor Mark Hamill, the original Luke Skywalker himself, alongside a group of dancing storm troopers; Skywalk is a glass paneled walkway at the top of the Rock, which provides unspoilt views straight down the near vertical drops from the peak of Gibraltar to the ground. If you suffer with vertigo, it may be best to bypass this installation.

39. Star Bar

The oldest bar in Gibraltar, a trip to the Rock would not be complete without swinging by Star Bar. Located in Parliament Lane, which connects Main Street to Irish Town, this establishment is billed as the oldest legal watering hole in Gibraltar; with local legend claiming that Christopher Columbus once stopped by to enjoy a meal before leaving to discover the Americas. Although the Star Bar is the oldest in Gibraltar, its décor is modern and, although not in keeping with the reputation of the pub, ensures that the bar appeals to modern patrons.

40. Bobby on the Beat

Gibraltar's policemen still wear the Dixon of Dock Green or Custodian Helmet that has lost its place in the UK. The police, who do an excellent job at keeping Gibraltar's crime rate low and the Rock a safe place to be, are only happy to oblige tourists request for a photograph and their traditional headgear make for a unique souvenir.

>TOURIST

41. Red Telephone Boxes

Another traditional sight that has disappeared from the streets of the UK, yet remains a permanent fixture in Gibraltar are the Red Telephone Boxes, designed by Sir Giles Gilbert Scott. If you're walking into Gibraltar from Spain, the first one that you will see will be on your right as you exit Customs, though this is not the best for a photo opportunity. There'll be one more by the Sundial Roundabout as you cross the runway on the right-hand side but the classic Gibraltar photograph involving the K6 versions of these booths, is to be taken as you walk from Grand Casemates Square onto Main Street. A duo of the classic red British design icons is to be found here and there will often be a queue to take a snap. The only problem with the telephone boxes is that, should you actually need to use one, you will find yourself in such a large queue of people lining up for a photograph of them pretending to use the booth, that you will be waiting for quite some time.

Stephen Philips

42. Europort

A nucleus of business activity, you'll find many high-rise office and residential building here. It's worth noting that, due to the proximity of the runway of Gibraltar airport, the buildings that you see are as tall as they're able to be by law. Catering to the office workers, you'll find cafes, fast food restaurants and a hypermarket here. Behind the supermarket, however, is a park that is bordered by the sea itself, where you'll have a good view of the docks and Algeciras in Spain across the Bay. There are picnic benches, play areas for the kids, exercise equipment and shaded areas all within the park.

43. American Steps

The American War Memorial is a World War I memorial, which was incorporated into Gibraltar's City Wall, the Line Wall Curtain, in 1937. Designed by French architect Paul Philippe Cret, and built between 1932 and 1933, it was, as is stated over the arch that leads to steps that take you down towards Midtown, "erected by the United States of America to

>TOURIST

commemorate the achievements and comradeship of the American and British Navies in this vicinity during the World War." On the other side of the monument, are two large bronze medallions: The Seal of the United States and of its Department of the Navy.

44. Windsor Suspension Bridge

One of the more recent attractions in Gibraltar, Windsor Suspension Bridge stretches for seventy-one metres over a fifty metre deep gorge high up in the Upper Rock Nature Reserve. Should you be able to keep your eyes open as you cross the bridge, you'll have views of the Strait on the western side of the Rock.

45. Pillars Of Hercules Monument

The Rock of Gibraltar, Calpe Mons, as well as its counterpart on the other side of the Strait, Abila Mons, together make up the Pillars of Hecules; the gateway to the Mediterranean Sea. At the monument built in celebration of the legend of Hercules and how he formed the pillars, you'll be able to listen in on tour guides recounting the legend itself and enjoy the spectacular views out across towards Africa. It's a photo opportunity up at the entrance to the Upper Rock Nature Reserve that should not be missed.

46. Tax Free Goods

One of the main draws of Gibraltar, you'll note a plethora of diamond, electronic, perfume, cigarette and alcohol shops all over Gibraltar. All of the jewelers and perfume sellers are prepared to haggle and you may save a pretty penny by buying some of your items here. One thing to note is that there are maximum purchase limits that you're able to make without declaring these at the border with Spain and cigarette and alcohol purchases in particular are tightly controlled.

47. Local Dish

The local cuisine of Gibraltar is a reflection of the people that have come to call the Rock home. 'Calentita', which lends its name to an annual food

>TOURIST

festival taking place in Casemates each June, means 'warm' in a familiar, cosy sense and is a baked pancake-like dish, similar to Algerian Calentica or Italian Farinata. Rosto is another local dish, which is a pasta and meat dish in a tomato and white wine sauce as is Callos. Advertised in several bars in town, Callos is a tripe stew, also containing chickpeas blood sausage or chorizo and bell peppers.

48. Casinos

In Ocean Village, you'll find two casinos, which offer Roulette, Blackjack and Poker tables, slot machines and even Bingo. To be enjoyed responsibly, once you've had your fill of gambling, you will be able to eat and drink and the bars and restaurants that are also housed within the premises. Open long after many of the bars close, should you not want to go to a nightclub, the casinos provide you with an alternative destination.

Stephen Philips

49. Live Music & Music Festival

Each year in September, usually to coincide with National Day (10th September), Gibraltar hosts a major music festival, drawing a number of local and international artists. Known as GMF (Gibraltar Music Festival) or Gibraltar Calling, thousands of festival goers descend on the Rock for two days of music, which fill Victoria Stadium, the multipurpose stadium that you will see on your right-hand side just after you have crossed the runway on your way into Gibraltar from Spain. Mainly used to host football matches (although the stadium also has an athletics track), the stadium is, however, unable to host Gibraltar National Team (who has a souvenir shop in Irish Town) matches, since it is not quite up to UEFA standards for international matches (although it does meet UEFA Category 2 standards and hosts UEFA intercontinental club matches). Instead the Gibraltar Football Association plays their 'home' international games a four hour drive away, through Spain into Portugal in Faro on the Algarve coast.

>TOURIST

Getting back the festival, hotels fill up quickly around this time, so it is important to book in advance.

One of many music festivals that take place on the Rock, there is also an annual Electronic Music Festival to name but one more. World renowned DJs are regularly flown in throughout the summer months and, in various bars in both Casemates and Ocean Village, you'll find live music every week.

50. Three Kings' Cavalcade

On the evening of 5th January each year, the Three Kings, who traditionally give Christmas gifts to all good boys and girls across the frontier in Spain make a stop off on the Rock in a procession which culminates in a ride through Main Street and Casemates Square throwing sweets out into the crowds that line their route. If you're on the Rock at this time of year, don't miss out on all of the fun and don't forget to bring something in which to store your loot.

Stephen Philips

TOP REASONS TO BOOK THIS TRIP

Views: The only place in the world where you can see two countries, two continents and two colonies. The vistas from the top of the Rock are second to none. On a clear day, you're able to see for miles and there's nowhere else on Earth you are going to see comparable views.

Culture: A real melting pot of European and Arabic heritage, it's possible to see a multitude of influences and styles in such a small, friendly place. Crime is low and this tightly-knit community welcomes visitors and foreign workers with open arms.

Location: A great place to spend a break and the perfect spring board to explore, south-western Europe or North Africa. The famous beaches of Tarifa, the southernmost point of Continental Europe, where the pace of life is so laid back that people are horizontal and where windsurfing, surfing and kite surfing are possible, are less than an hour away. An hour's drive east will get you to Marbella, the so-called millionaire's playground on the Costa del Sol. Cadiz and Jerez an hour and a half away and the Andalusian capital of Seville is two hours' drive.

Stephen Philips

>TOURIST

Read other Greater Than a Tourist Books

Greater Than a Tourist San Miguel de Allende Guanajuato Mexico: 50 Travel Tips from a Local by Tom Peterson

Greater Than a Tourist – Lake George Area New York USA: 50 Travel Tips from a Local by Janine Hirschklau

Greater Than a Tourist – Monterey California United States: 50 Travel Tips from a Local by Katie Begley

Greater Than a Tourist – Chanai Crete Greece: 50 Travel Tips from a Local by Dimitra Papagrigoraki

Greater Than a Tourist – The Garden Route Western Cape Province South Africa: 50 Travel Tips from a Local by Li-Anne McGregor van Aardt

Greater Than a Tourist – Sevilla Andalusia Spain: 50 Travel Tips from a Local by Gabi Gazon

Greater Than a Tourist – Kota Bharu Kelantan Malaysia: 50 Travel Tips from a Local by Aditi Shukla

Children's Book: Charlie the Cavalier Travels the World by Lisa Rusczyk

Stephen Philips

> TOURIST
GREATER THAN A TOURIST

Visit GreaterThanATourist.com:

http://GreaterThanATourist.com

Sign up for the Greater Than a Tourist Newsletter:

http://eepurl.com/cxspyf

Follow us on Facebook:

https://www.facebook.com/GreaterThanATourist

Follow us on Pinterest:

http://pinterest.com/GreaterThanATourist

Follow us on Instagram:

http://Instagram.com/GreaterThanATourist

Follow on Twitter:

http://twitter.com/ThanaTourist

Stephen Philips

> TOURIST
GREATER THAN A TOURIST

Please leave your honest review of this book on Amazon and Goodreads. Thank you. We appreciate your positive and constructive feedback. Thank you.

Stephen Philips

\>TOURIST

NOTES

Printed in Great Britain
by Amazon